3001200009910P

W9-AUS-307

FIRE!

WHEATLAND SCHOOL
24024 W. 103RD ST.
NAPERVILLE, IL 60564

FIRE!

BY JOY MASOFF

PRINCIPAL PHOTOGRAPHY
BY JACK REZNICKI
AND BARRY D. SMITH

SCHOLASTIC REFERENCE

This book is dedicated to every man and woman who has ever answered the call of a fire siren or the cry of a person in need.

Copyright © 1998 by Joy Masoff
All rights reserved. Published by Scholastic Inc.
SCHOLASTIC and associated logos are trademarks and/or registered trademarks of Scholastic Inc.

No part of this publication may be reproduced, or stored in a retrieval system, or transmitted in any form or by any means, electronic, mechanical, photocopying, recording, or otherwise, without written permission of the publisher. For information regarding permission, write to Scholastic Inc., Attention: Permissions Department, 555 Broadway, New York, NY 10012.

Library of Congress Cataloging-in-Publication Data

Masoff, Joy
Fire! / by Joy Masoff; principal photography by Jack Reznicki and Barry D. Smith.
p. cm.
Includes bibliographical references and index.
Summary: Presents the work done by firefighters, including the equipment they use, the fires they fight, the rescues and investigations they perform, and the history and future of fire fighting.
ISBN 0-590-97872-1
1. Fire extinction—Juvenile literature. [1. Firefighters.
2. Fire extinction. 3. Occupations.] I. Reznicki, Jack, ill. II. Smith, Barry D., ill. III. Title.
TH9148.M326 1998
363.37—dc21
                                        97-10928
                                             CIP
                                              AC
10 9 8 7 6 5 4 3 2 1   8 9/9 0/0 01 02 03

Printed in the U.S.A.   09
First printing, February 1998

FIRE!

A WORD OF INTRODUCTION

Why I Fought Fires 6

WHY FIRE BURNS

Know the Enemy 8

TOOLS OF THE TRADE

12 Things Every Firefighter Needs ... 10

All About Turnout 12

Start the Engines 14

Turn on the Hose 16

What They Use When They Can't
Use a Truck 18

The Jaws of Life 20

ON THE JOB

Different…Yet the Same 22

Answering the Call 24

Incredible Rescues 26

Smoke Jumpers & Hotshots 28

Firefighters & the EMS 30

Fire Detectives 32

What Does It Really Feel Like? 34

FIREFIGHTING PAST AND FUTURE

The Bucket Brigades 36

They Fought More Than Fires 38

Unforgettable Blazes 40

What Lies Ahead? 42

YOU CAN FIGHT FIRES…NOW!

12 Things You Can Do
Right Now 44

If You'd Like to Learn More 46

Photo Credits 47

A Note From the Author 47

Index 48

Why I Fought

I have always thought that being a firefighter is a special sort of blessing. In the thousands of alarms I have responded to and the many hundreds of fires I have fought, I was one of a particular group of people who did something so dramatic, so exciting, and so very necessary that I believe no other endeavor in life could have given me as much happiness and satisfaction.

To ride on a fire truck as it responds to an emergency is as exciting as any roller-coaster ride, but it is very serious business. Where would the world be if there were no firefighters? It is like asking where we would be without the police force or the military or even the government, for the world needs brave people to protect us if the human family is to survive. We cannot predict or prevent all emergencies, but we can protect against them, and firefighters are always in the front line of that defense.

I welcome this book and salute Joy Masoff for writing it, for it tells the firefighters' story in a unique and unforgettable way. When you have read this book, you will know how fires start, how they burn, how the firefighters get to the fire, and what equipment they use. You will see them in action and be able to imagine what it would be like fighting fires beside them.

I will always remember my first fire. That feeling of excitement mixed with awe is with me to this day.

Fires

BY DENNIS SMITH

The world of firefighting is changing, and now there are fire helmets that allow a firefighter to see through the thickest smoke when looking for victims. Yet firefighting remains ever the same, for the best way to fight a fire is still to get as close as possible to it and to cool it with water, quickly, for a fire can double its volume every minute. It takes a special group of trained, dedicated people to do this.

There are 35,000 fire departments in the United States and about 1.5 million firefighters. I hope someday soon you will stop by your own fire department to meet some of these heroic men and women.

Dennis Smith

Dennis Smith is a retired New York City firefighter, author of Report from Engine Company 82 and the founder of Firehouse Magazine

There is something almost alive about a fire. It needs food, it reacts to heat and cold, and it takes in oxygen. And when you're trying to put it out, a fire even seems to have a mind of its own. In order to stop a fire, firefighters need to know exactly what keeps it alive.

Know the Enemy

RECIPE FOR DISASTER

How does a fire happen? Well, for one thing, it takes the right ingredients. Just as there is no cake without flour, sugar, and baking powder, there is no fire without three things—FUEL, OXYGEN, and HEAT.

In the forest, trees and bushes are fuel for a fire. Where people live, a house framed with wood and full of furniture, books, and papers is like a huge feast for a hungry flame.

Oxygen is all around us, part of the air we breathe. If we didn't have oxygen, we wouldn't have fire, but then we wouldn't have people, either.

But trees and houses do not catch on fire simply by standing in the air. Without heat, the recipe is not complete.

HOT STUFF

When cake batter reaches about 350° Fahrenheit, it begins to change to a solid. When wood reaches 572°, it starts to give off a gas. That gas reacts with the oxygen in the air to make a flame. As the flame heats the remaining wood, the fire grows stronger. Even on the coldest day, if wood is heated to 572°, a fire will happen. The temperature at which something will ignite is called its FLASH POINT.

MATCH MAGIC

Wood can't get to 572° by itself. It needs help. Lightning can do it, or a spark from a campfire. And one little invention—the match—has given countless fires a leg up.

A match is a small stick of wood or pressed paper that has been dipped in a mixture of chemicals. Safety matches are usually coated with sulphur and potassium chlorate. A strip of red phosphorus is what the match is struck across. Every substance has its own flash point, and red phosphorus's flash point is very low, only 392°. When the red phosphorus hits its ignition point it sets off a chain reaction and causes the match to burst into flame.

But 392° is still a lot warmer than room temperature. Even a match needs a heat boost to catch fire. It gets that boost from friction. If you rub your hands together very quickly, you'll feel how much they warm up. That's friction. When a person rubs a match head quickly along the rough surface on the matchbox, the friction raises the temperature enough that the phosphorus catches fire. Then the flame from the burning phosphorus heats the wood or paper until it too bursts into flame.

Think of Fire as a Triangle

It requires three elements:

FUEL—something that burns
HEAT—an open flame, spark, radiated heat, electrical current
OXYGEN—one of the gases that makes up our air

Take one away and there cannot be a fire.

MORE THAN MEETS THE EYE

When you see a fire, you're seeing only one part of what's happening. There are really four parts to a fire—and all of them are dangerous.

FIRE GAS—The gases created by the process. You can't see them, but they are there...poisons such as carbon monoxide spreading through the air.

FLAME—The light given off by the burning gas. As long as the temperature is high enough, fire "food" is there, and oxygen is swirling around, you will see that light.

HEAT—The part of the fire that you can feel and the part that burns your skin. It's measured in degrees. A typical fire burns at about 1,100°. Now, you've seen what 400° can do to your Thanksgiving turkey. Triple the heat and you begin to get the idea of the power of a real fire.

SMOKE—A deadly cloud of vapor mixed with a very fine powder of solid particles. Many of the injuries in fires are caused by inhaling smoke, which injures the lungs. That's why firefighters wear air packs and masks.

TOO HOT TO HANDLE

Certain combinations of the three fire ingredients can lead to big troubles for firefighters. High heat can make a lot more than just wood burn—plastic and even some metal can catch fire or help to take the flames for a ride to another part of the house. Too much "food" and the fire quickly gets "fat" and starts to burn over a huge area. Too much oxygen, in the form of big winds, can push the fire over vast areas. As it is pushed, it finds more fuel. Before you know it, the fire is out of control, spreading faster than it can be put out. Its temperature might even hit 1,300°.

WARNING! WARNING! WARNING!

Any fire, however small, can be deadly. Think about what the poisonous gases and smoke can do to your body. Know that the flames will burn your skin (and if you've ever burned your finger on a hot stove you know what *that* feels like). Never, ever play with a match or try to put out a fire by yourself. Remember, fire has a mind of its own and it can twist and turn on you before you know what's hit you. Fire is never a joke.

TALK LIKE A FIREFIGHTER

FLASHOVER

Very scary. It's what happens when the air in a room becomes so hot that all the stuff—the bookcases, the sofa, the tables, the TV, *everything*—bursts into flame in one massive explosion.

BACKDRAFT

Fires breathe, and the harder they burn, the more air they use up...just like you when you run a mile. In a building fire, when the oxygen in a room is almost used up, the fire starts "gasping" for air; the flame dies down and the room fills with smoke. If you open the door to that room at that moment, the fire sucks in the oxygen so hard, the fire gases explode. The force can blow a person clear across the street.

FLASH POINT

The temperature at which a substance catches fire. Paper burns at 451° Fahrenheit. Socks won't burn until the temperature hits closer to 600°. Everything, even iron, has a flash point.

HEAT OXYGEN FUEL

Stay low to the ground if you are caught in a fire. Crawl out on your hands and knees. If your clothes catch on fire,

REMEMBER: STOP, DROP, & ROLL

It's difficult to build a house without bricks and wood or nails and a hammer. Firefighters need the right tools and equipment, too. Without these it's almost impossible to safely stop a blaze or handle a rescue. These are the items they depend on.

12 Things Every Firefighter Needs

1. Helmet and Hood

Originally made of leather, helmets today are made of Kevlar and high-impact plastic. A hard outer shell (and sometimes a mask) shields face and eyes. Fireproof flaps protect ears and neck. A fireproof hood goes underneath.

2. Airpack and Mask

Called an **SCBA**, for **S**elf-**C**ontained **B**reathing **A**pparatus. It holds 15 to 30 minutes of air.

3. Flashlight

It's dark in there… and smoky, too. Special flashlights show the way.

4. Rope

Can hold up to 9,000 pounds (about the weight of two cars). When the stairs are gone, this may be the only way out.

5. Fire Tool

There are lots of different fire tools. This one is great for testing damaged floors and walls. By banging the handle against the floor, firefighters find weak spots. With the ax-blade end of the tool, they make holes in the outside of the building to cool the fire and remove debris.

WHEATLAND SCHOOL
24024 W. 103RD ST.
NAPERVILLE, IL 60564

6. Boots

Stepping on a nail is always a danger. Made of rubber or leather, these are steel reinforced, puncture proof, and fire resistant.

7. Alarm

Firefighters call this a "pal," but its real name is a PASS, which stands for Personal Alert Safety System. If a firefighter stops moving, it's likely that he or she is hurt or trapped. The PASS senses that the firefighter isn't moving and makes a high-pitched noise to let others know something is wrong.

8. Walkie-Talkies

The firefighter is inside. The trucks are outside. The inside crew uses these to tell the others how big the fire is and how many hoses are needed.

9. Turnout Coat

Layers of space-age materials make these waterproof, heat proof, even acid proof. (See pp. 12–13.)

10. Bunker Pants

Almost four pounds of protection. No wonder they need suspenders to hold them up.

11. A Buddy

A trained firefighter never works alone.

WHEATLAND SCHOOL
24024 W. 103RD ST.
NAPERVILLE, IL 60564

12
Common
Sense

All About

You wouldn't go out to play in the snow and ice in a bathing suit, would you? Just as you depend on gloves, a hat, a warm coat, and boots to protect you, firefighters depend on their turnout gear. That gear can mean the difference between a successful rescue and disaster.

HELMET

HOOD
(Underneath helmet)

AIR CYLINDER

WALKIE-TALKIE (Worn on left side of coat)

PRESSURE GAUGE
(Shows how much air is left in the tank)

FIRE-RESISTANT LINED GLOVES

GEAR POCKET

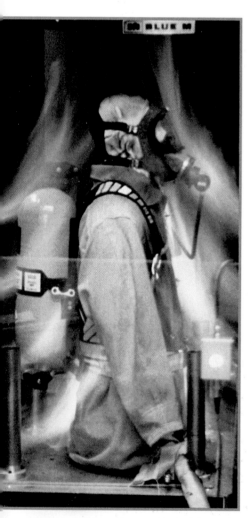

How can firefighters be sure their turnout can take the heat? By aiming eight blowtorches at it! Actually, firefighters don't do this, but the people who make the gear do. Layers of special flameproof fabric keep the flames out.

Total weight of the average turnout gear: 68 pounds!

BOOTS

Turnout

- —EYE SHIELD
- —FACE MASK
  (Underneath
  eye shield)

- —REGULATOR
  (Controls the flow
  of air in and out)

- —FIRE
  TOOL

- —BUNKER
  PANTS

▲ *A visitor from outer space? No.
Just a firefighter suited up in special
haz-mat gear. Depending on the
problem, there are three levels of
protective gear to choose from.*

WHAT THEY WEAR WHEN TURNOUT ISN'T ENOUGH

Putting out a house fire is one thing. But what happens when a big truck starts leaking acid or oil all over the road or a poisonous gas fills the air?

HAZ-MAT GEAR

Cleaning up a chemical spill is a lot like working in outer space. Without special clothing, you wouldn't last one second. Firefighters pull on special HAZ-MAT suits. Haz-mat is short for **haz**ardous **mat**erials. Every bit of the body must be completely covered, and the suit must be airtight. The suit must have no holes and no exposed seams. Places such as wrists, where air might sneak in, have clamps for a tight fit.

CLEANUP KITS

When the firefighters are suited up they'll need a few more items. Here are some things they might take with them:

AIR MONITOR—Is the air dangerous? Firefighters can find out with this neat gizmo. They hold it up and it tells which nasty chemicals and gases are in the air.

CHEMICAL CLASSIFIERS— Firefighters get a sample of a spill and dip these strips in it. The way the strips react helps the firefighters figure out what kind of spill it is.

DIKES—Look like giant stuffed snakes. Work like a superstrong roll of paper towels.

PILLOWS AND SHEETS—Not for sleeping, but great for mopping up toxic leaks because they are filled with special spongelike stuff.

PLUG-RUGS—These are perfect for patching a hole in the side of a leaking truck or a tank.

STORAGE DRUM—Firefighters toss those used dikes and pillows into this airtight container.

PORTABLE SHOWER AND DECON POOL— Bath time! The haz-mat suit has to be hosed off before it can be put away.

◄ *Airport firefighters wear special foil suits called **SILVERS** that can withstand 1,000° heat for short periods of time. With their silvers on, they can run into a burning airplane and pull people out.*

Start the Engines

We've all watched fire trucks screaming down the streets, sirens wailing and lights flashing. Ever wonder what each of those trucks actually does when it gets to the scene? These trucks, which firefighters call **APPARATUS** (ap-uh-**rat**-uhss), have important jobs to do.

▲ PUMPER

Pumpers use air to shoot out a powerful stream of water. Imagine a really powerful fan forcing the water through the hoses. In one minute these rigs can pump up to 1,500 gallons. That's like filling 50 bathtubs in just 60 seconds. (See pp. 16–17.)

◄ RESCUE TRUCK

Since so many calls involve accidents, these come equipped with all the things firefighters need to pull someone out of a dangerous situation. (See pp. 20–21 and 26–27.)

HAZ-MAT ►

When there is an oil or chemical spill or release, the air can become dangerous to breathe and the soil can become polluted. Animals and people can get sick. Firefighters need special equipment to keep the spill from spreading. Haz-mats carry that equipment. Inside, they have **BOOMS**, which look a lot like strings of giant cotton balls, to absorb the spills. Haz-mat rigs even have showers on board to wash off the poisons that get on firefighters' suits. (See p. 13.)

▲ SNORKEL

Instead of sending a person up a huge ladder with a hose, firefighters can use a snorkel truck. This truck has a long tube with the hose already inside it, controlled from the ground. And snorkels have another neat feature. The tubes can bend in the middle and extend over rooftops to reach the center of a building.

▲ THE CHIEF'S CAR

The fire chief is the big boss at the scene. Each truck has an officer in charge, but the chief is in charge of the officers. A chief always has a special car equipped with a complete communications system, so if more help is needed, it can be called in.

▲ AMBULANCE

Frequently, the fire department responds when calls reporting medical emergencies come in. Well-equipped ambulances stand at the ready, every shelf packed with life-saving equipment. (See pp. 30–31.)

▼ AERIAL

When a fire is burning in a tall building, firefighters can't just take the stairs. They may be full of smoke and flame. The best way to get inside is to climb up from the outside. Built-in ladders can extend up to the height of a ten-story building. Firefighters can then climb up and safely vent the smoke and heat from the outside, as well as help people down to safety.

Have You Ever Seen a Purple Fire Truck?

Who says fire engines have to be red?

Many departments have picked other colors…anything from white to neon green to banana yellow. There's even a purple truck in Columbia, MO.

If you took the amount of hose that the average pumper truck carries and laid it out in a straight line, it would extend for almost half a mile. But even the longest, thickest hose is useless unless the firefighters holding it know how to handle it and understand what kind of fire they are facing. Here are the basics.

Turn on

WATER, WATER EVERYWHERE

When the trucks arrive on the scene, the crews quickly get to work. All pumper trucks come with special hoses called ATTACK LINES. These hoses are about 1½ inches wide and are attached to the truck, always ready to use. All trucks also have built-in water tanks so that pumping can begin instantly. Within 30 seconds a team can be dousing the flames at full force. The "heat" leg will be broken by cooling the temperature. (See p. 9.)

THE HOSE KNOWS

The driver of the pumper quickly hooks up a second kind of hose, called an INTAKE LINE, to a fire hydrant or other water source (such as a tanker or a small pond—even a swimming pool). These hoses can be pretty big (up to five inches). DISCHARGE LINES, which average about three inches in diameter, can now be run to bring more water to the fire. But since these hoses are bigger and heavier than the intake lines, they may need several people to handle them.

ALL PUMPED UP

Pumper trucks are hard workers. Up to six hose lines can be run from one truck. The longer the hose, the more force is necessary to move the water along. If a hose is being pulled up stairs, it also will need more pressure. The driver's job is to control the pressure. The dials on the trucks tell what's happening with each hose. If there are no hydrants, a tanker truck will come and unload its water into a PORTABLE TANK. As soon as it has done that, it will quickly go off to get more water. This water relay race keeps up until the fire is out.

VALVE TO OPEN
DISCHARGE
GATES

DISCHARGE
GATES

TANKER
CONNECTION

HYDRANT
CONNECTION

EMER. MEDICAL TECH.

the Hose

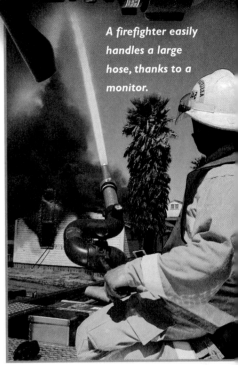

NOZZLE KNOW-HOW

The end of the hose line has a metal collar called the **NOZZLE**. Like a garden-hose nozzle, it has different settings to choose from. A soft mist of water that covers a big area is called a **FOG**, and it's used when a fire is coming toward the firefighter. Because it covers a broad area, it will keep the fire from wrapping around.

An **OPEN STREAM** sends water full force through the hose, but it targets a smaller area. Firefighters might use that setting at the end of the fire, when they are making sure all the flames have been put out. With quick, short bursts they will hit spots that they think might still hold heat.

A firefighter easily handles a large hose, thanks to a monitor.

HOW TO HANDLE A HOSE

Firefighters don't always aim a hose right at the fire. Indoors, they often aim the water up at the ceiling. That's because heat rises. The water hitting the ceiling turns into a big steam bath and forms a minirainstorm over the whole room. It's best to run a hose in 15- to 30-second squirts, especially an attack hose. It's important that the water doesn't run out before the bigger hoses are hooked up.

A fully charged hose is wild to handle. It can take several firefighters to control it. Firefighters sometimes use **MONITORS**, heavy stands that hold the hose aimed at a fixed spot. That way they need fewer people to control it.

TRICK CANDLES

Ever had a birthday cake with candles that light again after you blow them out? Fires can be a lot like that. Firefighters may think they have put out a fire only to have it flare up again. After the fire is put out, a crew carefully checks and rechecks every inch, feeling surfaces with their bare hands for any lingering heat.

PRESSURE GAUGES

THROTTLE GAUGE

OPENS TANK

ELECTRIC TRANSFER VALVE

PUMP AND LINE DRAINS

What Does It Feel Like to Hold an Attack Line?

Ask your best friend to push against you as hard as possible. Now you push back with the same force. That's what it feels like. Something as big and strong as you (the full hose) is pushing against you. You have to lean in to keep from falling over.

What They Use When They Can't Use a Truck

Sometimes firefighters can't just hop in a pumper or rescue truck and drive on over to a fire or an accident scene. Sometimes the road simply ends at the edge of a steep cliff. Sometimes the fire is burning on board a ship stranded out at sea. Sometimes a person has fallen through the ice too far from the shoreline to reach by throwing a rope. What can firefighters do?

WETBIKES

This San Francisco firefighter is off to the rescue on a **PWC** (Personal Water Craft) or **WETBIKE**. In cities that have twisty stretches of coastline, firefighters use these speedy little water bikes because they are perfect for steering into tiny coves and inlets. Best of all, they have no propeller that can hurt a person in the water.

HOVERCRAFT

When firefighters need vehicles that can travel on water *and* land, they go for these. Hovercraft can be launched from the shore and head right out to sea. This saves time in two ways. A regular boat might need to steer clear of shallow areas. These don't. And when the victims have been rescued, the firefighters can pull right up to the rescue rig instead of carrying the victim from boat to shore to ambulance.

FIRE BOATS

Firefighters use water to put *out* fires, right? So why is it that some of the most destructive fires happen on the waterfront?

Many of our country's biggest cities grew in places that could easily be reached by boat. Huge piers were built at the water's edge. To keep the wood from rotting, builders cover piers with a thick layer of creosote, an oily substance that is highly flammable. All it takes is a cigarette carelessly tossed aside or a spark from a ship's engine. Boom! Fire! In big cities, specially equipped boats and crews always stand at the ready.

AIRPLANES

When fire rages over a large area, even a huge fleet of trucks may not be enough to stop the flames. So fire chiefs look to the skies. They call in small aircraft that maneuver easily to make the first hits and bigger planes that carry enormous amounts of fire retardants to follow. Though many firefighting planes carry chemicals to smother the fires, some carry water. Swooping down low over a lake or ocean, these planes can suck up 12,000 pounds of water in 10 seconds! The biggest danger? Too much air traffic in the skies over the fire area!

HELICOPTERS

Fire has broken out on the seventy-eighth floor of a skyscraper, and there are people trapped on the roof. A brush fire is burning in a canyon, and two hikers are trapped. These are the times firefighters take to the skies to get to the scene.

Helicopters don't get stuck in traffic. They don't need roads to get to a fire. They move fast and can go almost anywhere.

The tough part of helicopter flying is getting through heavy smoke. It's hard to see, and that can be very scary. The most difficult part for firefighters is knowing when they *can't* help. There is a famous saying that goes like this: There are old pilots. There are bold pilots. But there are no old, bold pilots.

AIRBOATS

A boat is great for getting across the water, but it can't travel through swamps or over ice. When winter comes, lakes and rivers freeze, but they don't always freeze all the way. People fall through the ice and need to be rescued, so firefighters must be able to get across the water all year long.

Airboats skim along the top of the water or the ice, pushed by a huge propeller. The tricky thing about an airboat is, it has no brakes. Drivers have to know when to cut the engine so they don't end up needing to be rescued themselves.

The Jaws
AND OTHER

A driver of a car has lost control and hit the side of a stone wall at high speed. The metal of the car has twisted so badly that the doors cannot be opened, and the steering wheel has pinned the driver to his seat. Firefighters sense that the car might explode at any second. They need to get the driver out—*fast!* But how?

The Jaws are so heavy it takes two firefighters to control them.

TIME IS RUNNING OUT

When seconds count, firefighters turn to a host of special tools. Each does an important job and each works with the others to save lives. The **JAWS OF LIFE** is the most famous, a big 50-pound can opener for a crushed car. Its powerful fingers can easily pry apart mangled metal. In just 10 minutes a skilled firefighter can remove all four doors and the roof of a car.

It got its name because it could snatch an accident victim out of the jaws of death. It was first invented to save race-car drivers, who are involved in high-speed crashes all too often, their cars mangled and twisted. Word of the Jaws' strength quickly spread to the fire service.

CUTTERS

The Jaws work by prying things open. **CUTTERS** work by cutting things apart. Cutters can cut through metal as easily as scissors snip your hair. In a car crash, firefighters might want to cut through a roof support to reach the victim. In airplane crashes they might have to cut through the thick metal of the plane to free trapped passengers.

CUTTERS

RAMS

A **RAM** is a strong pole that adjusts to different heights and holds things up. When a car is badly damaged, it is no longer stable, and sometimes firefighters have to cut a support that holds up the roof so they can get to a trapped victim. But they don't want the roof to fall down on the victim, so they use a ram. Rams are also used sometimes to hold up sagging stairs or floors in a building fire or collapse.

AIR GUNS

These slice through metal like a table knife cuts through butter. If there are no doors and firefighters need to slice straight through metal, they use these. Airplane fuselages and sides of railway cars are just two places these are used.

AIR GUN
RAM

# of Life
LIFESAVERS

Inflatables may look like big square balloons, but they are true lifesavers.

As seen through the "eyes" of a TIC, a mother and child wait for help...help that will now come because they have been located through the dense smoke.

INFLATABLES

A new office building is going up. During construction a worker is pinned under a huge slab of stone. It's far too heavy for anyone to lift it off him. How can it be moved?

Firefighters often use air power to lift heavy objects. The bags they use are a lot like very strong balloons. Thin enough to slide under a heavy object, when they are pumped up they're strong enough to lift the weight off a trapped person.

HEAT-SEEKING CAMERAS

The smoke is thick and black. Firefighters can't see anything, but they know someone is still trapped inside. A TIC (Thermal Imaging Camera) will lead them right to the victim. It "sees" heat, not light. In addition to finding people by their body heat, it reveals hidden pockets of fire behind walls and under floors.

What Does It Feel Like?

IS IT HARD TO HANDLE THE JAWS OF LIFE?

Try lifting a 50-pound bag of dog food the next time you're in the supermarket. Then try to aim one corner at a spot the size of a fingertip.

Different...

When a call comes in—whether it's a report of flames at a country farm or smoke on the forty-eighth floor of a skyscraper—firefighters feel the same emotions. What will it be like? Will I be able to help? But every town is different; every department does things a different way.

Small Towns...

They are dentists and shop owners, carpenters and teachers...that is, until the sirens pierce the air. Then, like any superhero, they change into something different. Swiftly pulling on their super-hero clothes (actually, their turnout gear), they drop whatever they are doing and rush to the scene of a fire or a rescue.

In small towns and villages there are few fires and few people to have accidents. It would cost too much to have a staff of 20 or 30 people on call all the time. But fires do happen, cars do crash, people do get hurt. That's where the volunteers come on the scene.

These men and women do not get paid for their work. They do it to help their towns. They learn their firefighting and rescue skills after work and on weekends. They flip pancakes and run carnivals to raise money to help buy new equipment. They scramble out of warm beds in the middle of the night and leave their jobs when they hear their beepers sound. It's a big sacrifice, and yet there are almost one million volunteer firefighters in the United States alone.

Yet the Same

They all have different names for their equipment and different systems for getting things done. In big cities, people get paid to be firefighters. In small towns, they usually don't. But one thing is the same. It's *always* challenging, always demanding…always thrilling.

and Big Cities

In places with hundreds of thousands of people to protect, calls for help come all the time. City firefighters stay at the station house, always ready, sometimes even sleeping there. And because they protect bigger buildings, they must have more specialized training.

Big-city firefighters face big challenges, such as putting out a fire on the sixtieth floor of a skyscraper filled with thousands of people, or rescuing hundreds of travelers from a smoke-filled train. They can answer a dozen calls a day, and because of the size of the fires they face, they run a very real risk of getting hurt.

They spend a lot of time trying to prevent fires by inspecting buildings and teaching people how to become fire-smart. And in really big cities there's an enormous amount to do. In New York, where there are almost eight million people, firefighters go out on more than 350,000 calls a year.

You are a firefighter. People count on you to come the moment they call. But you never know when that call will happen, so you are always ready. You check your equipment. You check your equipment again. You might sleep at the fire station a few nights each month or you might sleep in your house with a beeper at your bedside. But you always wait for that moment when you hear the call for help.

The station house is a second home to you. The people you work with are more than just your co-workers. They are the people you trust with your life. They have become like family—brothers and sisters you love fiercely, even if sometimes you get on one another's nerves.

You wait and check and practice. And then it happens....

Answering the Call

When the bells and buzzers sound in the station house, there is a great burst of activity. Poles are slid down, gear is pulled on. Firefighters call these runs **JOBS** or **WORKERS**. Let's pretend that for just one day, *you* are a big-city firefighter. You've got a worker!

No, these aren't pants for a very short person. These bunker pants are already tucked into boots, ready to be pulled on at a second's notice.

YOUR ASSIGNMENT: ENGINE 21

Unlike small-town fire departments, which keep all their equipment in one place, big-city fire departments keep their trucks in buildings all over town, just a few trucks to each building.

Each truck has a team. There's a **DRIVER** (who takes care of the rig), an **OFFICER** (who's in charge of the crew), and **FIREFIGHTERS** (who tackle the flames or mount the rescues). In the old days, those firefighters were called "back-steppers" because they used to ride on the back of the truck, hanging on for dear life. This was very dangerous, so new trucks carry them inside.

You will work on a shift—usually a 24-hour period when you live at the station, eating and sometimes sleeping there. Remember, fire doesn't take vacations. Accidents never take the night off.

LIFE IN THE HOUSE

When you arrive for your shift, you pull out your gear and get it set up near your rig. If you're going to be working at night, you make your bed and help clean up the station house. There are usually training sessions to attend. You might even shop for groceries and cook dinner. There's always a lot to do.

The calls will come in to DISPATCH via the 911 network, and you never know what they will be. A child locked in a bathroom, a car that hit a stop sign, a burst pipe, a funny smell, a cat stuck inside a wall…people call the fire department for help with *everything*.

Pull on your hood, pull on your mask, check the airflow, and head on in!

STRUCTURE FIRE, CORNER OF PARK AND MAIN

But a fire call is something special. And now, just before lunch, a call has come in. Smoke is billowing from a store downtown. You hear your truck number called. In many fire stations you slide down the pole and slide into your turnout gear. Then, with your heart racing, you hop on your rig.

ALL ABOARD

The sirens are on, the lights flashing. You're on your way. You try to imagine what's waiting for you, and all the time your mind is racing along with your heart. You feel excited. This is what you've trained for.

OUT OF CONTROL

When you get to the scene, the crew breaks up into teams. Some of you pull in the attack hoses to cool the flames. Some set the bigger discharge lines. Others are part of SEARCH AND RESCUE, looking for people or pets. Still others ventilate the building by breaking windows or cutting holes in the roof.

When it is all over and the fire is almost KNOCKED DOWN, you shovel up the cinders and toss outside anything that might still burn, then soak it until you can touch it with your bare hands. This is called the OVERHAUL.

The one word firefighters never want to hear is REKINDLE…a fire they thought was out but wasn't.

Three hours after the first alarm, it's back to the station, into a quick shower, and finally it's time for a very late lunch.

EAT LIKE A FIREFIGHTER
Firefighter McNulty's Four-Alarm Chicken

Ask a grown-up to help you whip up this reheat-and-eat dinner. Serves an entire firehouse (6–8 people)

- ☑ 4 cups cut-up boneless chicken breasts
- ☑ 2 cups celery, thinly sliced
- ☑ ¼ cup chopped green pepper
- ☑ ¼ cup chopped red pepper
- ☑ 2 tsps. lemon juice
- ☑ 1½ cups spaghetti sauce
- ☑ 1 cup bread crumbs
- ☑ 1 tablespoon melted butter
- ☑ 1 cup grated cheddar cheese

For a spicier dish add 1½ tbsps. Worcestershire sauce and 1 tsp. Tabasco sauce.
Combine all the ingredients except the bread crumbs, butter, and cheese. Pour into a baking dish. Top with grated cheese. Toss the bread crumbs with melted butter and sprinkle over the top. Bake at 350° for 40 minutes. Can be reheated whenever a rescue interrupts.

Incredible

Every day the calls come in. A building collapse. A car off a bridge. A child trapped in a cave. And every day firefighters risk everything to bring people to safety. Being a firefighter involves so much more than putting out fires.

You don't just wake up one day and decide that you are going to save people. Firefighters train long and hard, learning skills that they pray they will never have to use. When a call for help does come in, they set off with hearts racing, their minds working at lightning speed. This is what they face....

SWIFT-WATER RESCUES

A flash flood can happen anytime and anyplace. Before you know it, a car can be swept away by a wall of water, its driver and passengers helpless to do anything to stop it. Swift-water rescues are always quick rescues. The rescue crew must move *fast* or it will be too late.

Cold water lowers body temperature, leaving a person weak. A lifeline thrown to someone who can't hold it isn't of much use. Staying afloat in rushing water takes a lot of energy and strong currents can pull you under. A firefighter has to get down and help.

This firefighter, hanging by a rope from the ladder of his aerial truck, has managed to grab this man just as his pickup is swept under water.

▲ ROPE RESCUES

Everyone has some rope lying around the house. Quite a handy little item. And in the hands of a skilled rescuer it can save a life.

Teamwork is the key to a rope rescue. Using pulleys and other specially designed hardware, even a small person can help pull up an injured victim.

Rescues

◀ CONFINED-SPACE RESCUES

Imagine being squeezed in a tiny tube. You can't move your arms or legs. You can hardly breathe. You are completely stuck. Sewers, pipelines, grain silos...you'd be surprised how often people get stuck in tight places.

Ropes play a big part in this type of rescue, but there are other twists. Firefighters need light and air along with extremely narrow special stretchers called **SKEDS**. Slithering through a tight space with an air cylinder on your back is tough. Getting a victim back out is even tougher. The sked, hooked to ropes that link up to the surface, makes it possible.

◀ COLLAPSE RESCUES

When earthquakes strike or fire weakens a building, walls can give way and roofs can cave in, trapping people inside. Some fire departments have highly trained Urban Search and Rescue Teams, called USARs.

They depend on special equipment. Video cameras on the end of long flexible poles and trained dogs that can smell trapped victims help USARs find people who are buried under layers of rubble. And they know how to keep things from getting worse, how to lift heavy beams and concrete without having the buildings collapse even more.

◀ CAVE & MINE RESCUES

Deep within the earth, passageways are sometimes almost too narrow for a person to fit through. It is cold and damp, and it's easy to get lost.

Climbing skills are key here, as well as lots of special equipment—safety harnesses, ropes and pulleys, headlamps and hardwire headsets. Only one person can go down at a time, but it's not unusual for a cave rescue to take several days, so tag-teamwork is a must. When the victims are found, skeds will be brought down to help bring them to safety.

▼ IN-WATER RESCUES

A car slides off a bridge. A skater falls through the ice. Amazingly, a person can survive under very cold water for up to 20 minutes, because the cold slows down all the body functions.

Highly trained rescue divers wear dry suits and use small inflatable boats called **TENDERS**. They must move slowly—they don't want to stir up the murky bottom of the lake or river—but not too slowly because time is running out! Diving through pitch-black waters, when you can't even see your hand in front of your face, is a challenge. Underwater lights help, but the most important thing is to stay calm.

A dry suit is pulled right over street clothes. A full-face mask will completely cover eyes, nose, and mouth.

SAFETY LINE

FULL-FACE MASK

Smoke Jumpers & Hotshots

Slap the door, then slap the jumper's leg. It's time to jump.

It starts with the crackle of lightning deep in the woods or a campfire carelessly put out. Dry summer heat has baked the air; rain has been scarce. A sudden gust of wind fans the smoldering embers, and within minutes a deadly fire blazes. From high above, in lookout towers, fire spotters scan the horizon for telltale plumes of smoke. And when the fire call comes in, within minutes planes will be airborne with special teams of firefighters.

SMOKE JUMPERS...FIRST ON THE SCENE

Fighting a forest fire is very different from fighting a structure fire. The U.S. Forest Service, faced with the task of protecting thousands of acres of wilderness, must sometimes extinguish blazes that rage over miles and miles. Smoke jumpers are specially trained firefighters who begin the attack on a fire by leaping from airplanes because that's the fastest way (and sometimes the only way) to get to the scene. It's tough, hard work, and only the very strongest can do it.

HOTSHOTS—MUSCLE AND DETERMINATION!

The hotshots, the other fighting arm of the fire service, follow close behind, clearing makeshift roads and launching the major attack. They stay on the job for days at a time, grabbing a hasty meal or a short rest when they can. They are fiercely dedicated men and women, mostly college students and schoolteachers, willing to take incredible risks to protect our natural resources. This is how they put out a blaze.

SAFETY HELMET

ASBESTOS SHROUD

FIRE PACK WITH SURVIVAL GEAR (food, flashlights)

FIRE-RETARDANT JACKET

TWO-WAY RADIO

CANTEEN

FIRE SHELTER

DRIP TORCH

A plane heads for the heart of the flames, where it dumps a load of fire-stopping chemicals.

HOW DO YOU PUT OUT A FIRE WITHOUT WATER?

There are no fire hydrants in the forest, and you can't drive a tanker truck in. You have to stop the flames a different way. Fires need three things—oxygen, fuel, and heat—to burn. (See pp. 8–9.) Trees, brush, and leaves are all extremely flammable. Using a special tool called a PULASKI, hotshots and smoke jumpers clear wide paths in a large circle around the fire so that there is only dirt—not a branch is left. When the fire reaches the circle, it has no "food" and starves to death. If the fire is very large, planes and helicopters are sent to drop special chemicals that smother the flames. Deprived of oxygen, the blaze will die.

WHAT DO YOU LEARN AT SMOKE-JUMPER SCHOOL?

Caught in a tree on purpose, a hotshot cuts his way down and out.

Never parachuted before? That's good—the Forest Service prefers you to have never jumped out of a plane. As a veteran smoke jumper puts it, "Sky divers tend to show off and bring bad habits with them." Smoke jumpers learn to jump with the help of a four-story-high tower. After a dozen test flights, a jump is made into a thick stand of trees so the parachutes get caught. If students can get down safely, they're ready to fight a blaze.

ONLY THE STRONG SURVIVE

This is what it's like to work on the firelines. Imagine spending 10 to 18 hours a day in smoky brush, digging and clearing, with only a few short hours for sleep. It's exhausting work, yet far more people apply than can be hired. Why? As one hotshot put it, "This is the greatest job in the world. These are the greatest people in the world. These are the most beautiful places in the world. How can you beat that?"

This specially constructed fire shelter is used to show smoke jumpers and hotshots the correct position to lie in if they have to use their tents.

TALK LIKE A HOTSHOT

FIRELINE
A strip of land from which all brush and debris have been cleared to rob a wildfire of its fuel.

▲ SKY JELL-O
The pink, fire-retardant chemical dropped from planes to smother difficult fires.

▶ CHAINS
Sixty-six-foot-long sections of the fireline. This team will cut about 20 chains in an hour…sometimes working for 24 hours at a time.

◀ PULASKI
A combination ax and hoe, used to dig a fireline.

▼ SHAKE 'N' BAKE
Smoke jumpers really call them this! An aluminum foil and fiberglass tent, this is used *only* as a last resort. If the fire is under 1,000°, it will protect them. But some fires burn at 1,500° to 2,000°, and high winds can rip the tents apart. Smoke jumpers try very hard *not* to get into situations where they need to use them.

A young man painting the trim high up on the second story of his house loses his footing and falls from the ladder. A woman gardening with her grandson suddenly finds she can't breathe. A car skids on an icy roadway and crashes into a tree.

Within minutes help will be on the way.

Firefighters &

MORE THAN JUST FLAME STOPPERS

By now you know that firefighters do much more than just put out fires. Over three-quarters of the calls fire departments receive involve the Emergency Medical Service (EMS)…anything from a car accident to a sudden illness. Firefighters spend a lot of time learning how to save lives, and all have advanced first-aid training. When a call for help goes out, they are usually the first ones on the scene.

EMERGENCY MEDICAL TECHNICIANS

Many firefighters are Emergency Medical Technicians (EMTs). But what *is* an EMT? It's a person who can provide basic medical care from the scene of the accident all the way to the hospital. From putting pressure on a deep cut to starting a heart that has stopped—an EMT is trained to help. EMTs with advanced training are called PARAMEDICS.

COOL, CALM, AND IN CONTROL

The key to a successful rescue is being prepared. Equipment and supplies are checked and double-checked. Every second counts, and EMTs must respond to the scene quickly. But before they rush to aid the victim, they have to make sure the area is safe—that a car engine is not still running or in danger of catching on fire, for example. Getting to the victim can be hard. Sometimes a car is partially under water or its doors are smashed. Only when the accident scene is made safe can an EMT finally turn to the patient.

WHAT SHOULD YOU DO IF YOU COME ACROSS AN ACCIDENT SCENE?

REMAIN CALM—
Getting upset helps no one.
DON'T TRY TO MOVE THE PERSON—
You could make things worse.
CALL 911—
Tell the operator what has happened (for example, your friend fell skateboarding and is bleeding badly). Most 911 calls are traced automatically. The operator will know where you are calling from unless you are using a cellular phone. Stay on the line until the operator tells you to hang up.

the EMS

IS THE VICTIM BREATHING? BLEEDING?

At last it's time to help the victim. Are there broken bones? Is the person bleeding? Breathing? Quickly, confidently, EMTs always remember their ABCs. That stands for Airway—is something keeping the air from getting to the lungs? Breathing—are the lungs damaged? Circulation—does

the patient have a pulse, and is there a heartbeat?

Working as quickly as possible without putting the victim in danger, the firefighter carefully moves the victim to the rescue vehicle. If there are possible neck injuries, the victim will be strapped to a stiff board with the head cradled in a foam brace. If there is no breathing or pulse, rescue breathing and chest compressions (also called CPR, or cardiopulmonary resuscitation) will be started to keep oxygen going into the lungs and blood moving through the body.

THIS IS RESCUE 43. DO YOU COPY?

The patient is settled in the rescue vehicle. Using a two-way radio or a cellular phone, the EMTs contact the nearest hospital to report the patient's condition. That way, the emergency-room staff can be prepared. For example, if a person has a badly broken leg, the ER staff will make sure that the right specialist will be there. On the way to the hospital, the EMTs keep a careful eye on the patient and try to make him or her as comfortable as possible.

After the patient is at the hospital, the rescue rig has to be cleaned, a report filed, and supplies restocked. The next rescue might be only minutes away.

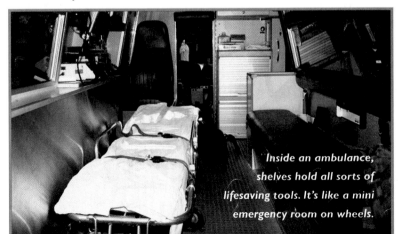

Inside an ambulance, shelves hold all sorts of lifesaving tools. It's like a mini emergency room on wheels.

WHAT'S INSIDE THE RIG?

WHAT'S WRONG WITH THE PATIENT?
BASIC SUPPLIES: stethoscope, penlight, blood-pressure cuff

WE'VE GOT TO MOVE THEM
THINGS TO LIFT AND MOVE: stretchers, stairchairs, long backboards, blankets, pillows.

HER LEG IS BROKEN
THINGS TO KEEP BROKEN BONES FROM MOVING: splints, padded boards, air-inflatable splints, neck braces, collars, slings

HE'S BLEEDING
SUPPLIES FOR WOUNDS: sterile pads, bandages, burn kits, sterile sheets, tape, scissors

HER HEART IS NOT PUMPING WELL
SUPPLIES FOR TREATING SHOCK: special pants that keep blood flowing to the brain instead of rushing to the legs. These are called MAST pants —short for Military Anti-Shock Trousers.

THE BABY SWALLOWED TOO MANY PILLS
POISON KIT: special syrups and drinks to bring on vomiting or to dilute poisons

THE CAR HAS FLIPPED OVER
RESCUE GEAR: chains, ropes, power tools, warning flares, searchlights

I MUST PROTECT MYSELF FROM INJURY
PROTECTIVE GEAR: disposable gloves, face masks, eye goggles, helmets, reflective vests

HE'S IN BAD SHAPE
ADVANCED-CARE SUPPLIES: devices that can restart a stopped heart, replace lost fluids, open up blocked airways

DO YOU COPY? OVER!
COMMUNICATIONS DEVICES: two-way radios, walkie-talkies, cellular phones

HE'S NOT BREATHING
OXYGEN TANKS

The Average Rescue Vehicle Carries Over 200 Different Items!

In the middle of the night a warehouse filled with sporting equipment bursts into flames. Within minutes the entire building is burning. The night watchman describes a noise that sounds like it might have been an explosion. As firefighters arrive on the scene, they begin to suspect that something about this fire just isn't right.

Fire Detectives

HALF FIREFIGHTER, HALF POLICE OFFICER

The fire burned hot and fierce. It took hours to put out. The crews are exhausted. But there is one important thing they still must do. When a fire department is finished putting out a blaze, the officer in charge must write up a report about it. And if anything seems a little odd, if a lot of property has been destroyed, if there have been injuries or lives lost, the case is immediately turned over to the FIRE MARSHAL's office and its team of trained investigators. Sifting through the wreckage and talking to eyewitnesses, they will begin to find out why this fire happened. These firefighters carry more than hoses and fire tools; they carry guns, too. That's because they are also sworn police officers with special law-enforcement training. They interview witnesses, collect evidence, make arrests, and finally appear in court to help send the criminals to jail.

They are called ARSON INVESTIGATORS.

FIRE SUSPICIOUS IN ORIGIN

Most fires are started by accident or carelessness...a cigarette forgotten as a man dozes on his couch, or a three-year-old playing with matches while her parents cook dinner. But sometimes a fire happens on purpose. The people who set these fires are called ARSONISTS, and the crime they have committed? ARSON! This is so horrible a crime that the federal government gets involved, bringing the full powers of this country to the pursuit and capture of these criminals.

SMOKE SCHOOL

Arson investigators must learn all about how fires are set. They learn about ACCELERANTS (ak-**sel**-uh-*rants*), which make fires burn hotter—chemicals such as gasoline and lighter fluid. They learn about DELAY DEVICES, fire starters, such as cigarettes, that take time to get a fire started. Arsonists use them so they have time to leave the building before it starts to burn. And by setting fires themselves in specially built fireproof training buildings, investigators learn how to spot a fire that has been set on purpose. They even learn how to leave false clues.

THE POINT OF ORIGIN

On the scene, they sift through the smoky rubble looking for small telltale signs such as V-shaped marks that show where the fire started. This spot always has the most burn damage because the fire burned there for the longest period of time. It is called the **POINT OF ORIGIN** and is of enormous interest to investigators.

FIRE FINGERPRINTS

Most experienced firefighters can tell almost instantly if a blaze was started on purpose. Sometimes the people who start a fire leave obvious clues at the scene of the crime. Sometimes they are very crafty and go to great lengths to hide their handiwork. But they are almost always caught.

WHY?

Why do people start fires? There are six different reasons: Half the arson arrests are for **VANDALISM**—destroying someone else's property to make the vandal feel powerful. Vandals might burn a church that belongs to a religion they do not agree with.

Some fires in empty buildings are set just for the **THRILL** of seeing the building burn. But that fun can hurt and even kill, and those thrill seekers can end up spending 30 years in jail. **REVENGE** is another reason fires are set. An arsonist might try to get even with someone by burning his or her property.

People who need money sometimes try to collect on their insurance policies by burning their own homes or offices for **PROFIT**. And to get the attention of the newspapers and TV, some people light a blaze in the name of **POLITICS**. Finally, sometimes arson is used **TO HIDE** the evidence of another crime, such as a robbery.

SMOKE SLEUTHS

Many arson investigations involve the Bureau of Alcohol, Tobacco and Firearms, which is called the **ATF** for short. This U.S. government agency sends out agents who are part of the Arson Task Force…*also* called the **ATF**. Every major city in the United States has an office where teams of agents work. The ATF also has CFIs, **CERTIFIED FIRE INVESTIGATORS**. These investigators have very specialized knowledge of the chemistry of how fires start and burn. They often work closely with the **FBI**, the Federal Bureau of Investigation.

DOGGY DETECTIVES

Arson investigators have help in their quest for answers. Some departments use specially trained dogs who are able to sniff out different types of accelerants. Knowing how the fire was started helps investigators find the criminal.

CAUGHT AND CAPTURED

Every scrap at the point of origin is examined. Even a small splinter can hold answers. In a very famous case, a tiny piece of yellow lined paper that had not been completely burned yielded one perfect fingerprint, a print that eventually led to an arrest. If gasoline is found at the scene, chemists can look at it under a microscope and discover what brand it is, sometimes even where it was bought. The numbers tell the story. In an average year, 2.3 million fires are reported. And of those, almost half have been started on purpose. But most of the fire starters are caught and sent to jail for a very long time.

Sifting through the rubble of a burned building, an Arson Task Force team searches for clues.

What Does It Really Feel Like?

Their truck number has just been called. They have 30 seconds to slide into their gear, hop aboard the rig, and head off toward the next mystery that awaits.

What goes through firefighters' minds on the way to a fire or rescue? They might ask themselves, "What will I find? Will I be able to help?"

Here are some of the questions *they* get asked.

Firefighters depend on their buddies to help them if they are injured.

Q. WHAT ARE YOUR WORST FEARS?

A. Getting tangled up in fallen wires, getting lost in the dark, getting caught in a building collapse or a flashover, getting nails through the bottoms of their boots. There is *so* much that can go wrong. Firefighters must learn to depend on their friends, their equipment, their intuition.

Q. HOW HOT DOES IT GET?

A. When you open an oven door to remove fresh baked cookies, that oven is heated to about 350° Fahrenheit. A fire burns almost three times hotter. Oddly enough, heavy turnout gear keeps firefighters from baking crisp as a cookie. Air cylinders are insulated, and every breath draws a cooling bath of compressed air across the face. The helmet and hood and turnout protect the skin. Sure the firefighters sweat, but that sweat helps to cool their bodies, too.

Firefighters learn quickly never to touch the metal buckles on a helmet or turnout with bare hands when they come out of a fire. They don't want to burn their fingers.

> There is nothing wrong with this picture. This is is what a firefighter might see as he or she nears the heart of the blaze.

Q. WHAT CAN YOU SEE WHEN YOU ARE IN A SMOKE-FILLED BUILDING?

A. Basically, nothing. Imagine smoke so thick you can't see your hand in front of your face...darkened stairwells that you can only grope your way up. Nothing you have seen in the movies can prepare you for the clouds of blinding smoke that surround you.

To get some idea of what it's really like, have someone blindfold you, and put on your backpack—full of books. Then try to crawl on your hands and knees from one side of your house to the other. Have your friend keep a close watch so you don't hurt yourself.

Q. DO YOU GET TIRED WHEN YOU ARE FIGHTING A BLAZE?

A. *Very.* But with all that energy pumping through their bodies, many firefighters don't realize it. They keep pushing long after they should have stopped to rest. In hot weather, when they are sweating a lot, it's easy to overdo it. Firefighters have to learn to listen to their bodies or they can easily end up needing the EMTs themselves.

Q. IS IT SCARY?

A. Fighting a fire is like going on a wicked roller-coaster ride at an amusement park. One part of your stomach is twisting with fear, but at the same time it's exciting and exhilarating and *thrilling*.

Q. WHAT DO YOU DO FOR FUN?

A. Things can get pretty tense when you don't know what your day will bring. Firefighters know that a silly prank comes in handy for letting off steam. Here are some favorites:

When a call comes in, street shoes come off, and boots go on. Many a time, a firefighter has returned from the job to find the toes of his or her shoes full of shaving cream or toothpaste.

Sleeping in the station offers all sorts of chances to play practical jokes. A favorite trick at one station involved an air-raid siren set to go off in the rafters above a new rookie's bed at 3 A.M. The turn-off switch was hidden under a layer of tape, and the rest of the crew were wearing ear plugs.

HOW DO YOU BECOME A FIREFIGHTER?

There are a lot of people who want to become firefighters. You have to pass a tough test to make the team. Here's what you need to do.

1. Drag a 50-foot, 80-pound hose for one block, then turn around and drag it back.
2. Fold a 46-pound hose over your shoulder and run up three flights of stairs, then lug it 85 feet.
3. Climb a 4½ foot wall.
4. Lift a 60-pound, 20-foot ladder, position it, and climb up, then down.
5. Crawl through a 25-foot-long tunnel, then drag a 145-pound dummy 45 feet across a finish line.

BETTER HURRY! YOU HAVE TO DO ALL THIS IN UNDER SIX MINUTES.

Guess what? You're not done yet. After that, there are strength tests (jumping, running, gripping) and a written test on fire science as well.

FIREFIGHTER GOLF?

No. Not exactly. Firefighters don't tee off after putting out a blaze. They use golf tees to plug leaks in gas tanks and storage drums.

In 1607, Jamestown, Virginia, became the first English settlement in America, and in 1608 it burned to the ground. Life in this "new world" seemed to be one big fire after another. Year after year people built homes only to see them go up in flames. Here's why....

The Bucket

THE FIRST LITTLE PIG BUILT HIS HOUSE OF STRAW

The first homes in our country were built quickly, using easily found materials such as brush, tree limbs, clay, and grasses. The roofs were made of thatch (which is made from bundles of straw lashed together) and mud. If you've ever been to a campfire, you know that a lot of those things make for a mighty flame. There was no heat or hot water and no electric stoves, so people kept fires going all day long in poorly constructed hearths. To make matters worse, many folks kept barrels of gunpowder and a good supply of whiskey nearby. Those are two of the most explosive things around. Most homes were a fire waiting to happen.

EVEN CHILDREN WERE FIREFIGHTERS

If you lived in the 1600s you would have been a part of the firefighting force. It took the whole town to stop a blaze. Every single home had a leather bucket hanging near the door just for putting out fires. Unlike today, when you just turn on a faucet to get water, townspeople had to get water from ponds, rivers, or wells. When a fire broke out, people formed a **BUCKET BRIGADE**. Two lines stretched from the town's water source, everyone armed with a bucket. The men would fill the buckets and pass them toward the fire; the women and children would send the empty ones back to be filled. Most times it was too little water, too late. Town after town burned to the ground.

IT'S 9 P.M. IS YOUR FIRE OUT?

Wisely, the elders knew things had to change. Laws were passed forbidding the use of flammable building materials such as thatch. And because most fires occurred at night, while people slept, their fireplaces still lit for warmth, a curfew (which comes from the French for "cover the fire") was ordered. You could not have a fire going between 9 P.M. and 4:30 A.M. If you broke the law, you paid a heavy fine, and the money went toward big buckets, ladders, hooks, and rope.

Brigades

When Ben Franklin wasn't flying kites in lightning storms, he was busy improving day-to-day life.

THE RATTLE WATCH

In the quickly growing cities, more and more houses were being built, all packed in close together. When one caught on fire, dozens ended up burning. In some cities, men were appointed to wander the streets at night to watch for fires. They carried big wooden rattles that made an alarming sound when twirled.

WHO INVENTED THE FIRE DEPARTMENT?

Benjamin Franklin, one of the greatest Americans ever, convinced a group of Philadelphia's leading citizens to band together to form the Union Fire Company. Willing to drop what they were doing to rush to the scene, they brought with them a great sense of dedication and loyalty—the true spirit of firefighting to this day. Franklin also published an important newspaper, and he frequently printed articles urging people to be more careful. He came up with the phrase "an ounce of prevention is worth a pound of cure" to keep people from carrying hot coals on shovels from room to room. George Washington, Paul Revere, and Thomas Jefferson were all volunteer firefighters, along with many other patriots. It was the right thing to do for a growing country.

YOU'RE IN GOOD HANDS...WITH HAND-IN-HAND

In the 1700s, if your house burned down, you would most likely depend on friends and relatives to help rebuild it and to offer temporary shelter. But what if those friends were short of cash, your relatives short on room? Wise Mr. Franklin knew there was a better way, so he created the first insurance company, which was eventually called the Hand-in-Hand Company.

It worked like this: You paid Hand-in-Hand a yearly fee. In exchange, they placed a small marker on your door. If your house caught fire, they would send a special fire brigade to the scene. If they could not save your house, they paid you enough money to rebuild it.

As the century drew to a close, most of America's cities had well-trained volunteer firefighters, and people took more care in the construction of their homes. There were primitive fire engines (actually big wooden tubs on a platform with wheels) and someone to help if your home did burn down. But those very things that made life so much better created a new set of problems.

It's easy to see why Jamestown, Virginia, kept burning down. The houses were made of campfire ingredients.

They Fought More Than Fires

Imagine having to duke it out before going to fight a fire. Well, that's exactly what began to happen in the 1800s.

HOT UNDER THE COLLAR

Ben Franklin's insurance company was so successful that other companies soon sprang up. With each company offering rewards to the first brigade to put out a blaze, a new problem arose. Often, to the horror of the homeowner whose house was burning, rival groups would fight each other for the honor of putting out the fire. Unfortunately, by the time the fighting was over, the house had usually burned to the ground.

STRONGER THAN A HORSE?

The 1800s were tough years in the history of firefighting, although there *were* great technical achievements. America's cities were growing bigger day by day, and this growth increased the demand for fire protection. But the new recruits tended to be rowdy and reluctant to even try the new inventions that would have made things easier for them. They simply preferred brute strength to common sense. In fact, they even refused to use horses to pull their heavy equipment. Maybe it was because they prided themselves on their muscles and considered it an insult to their physical abilities. Or maybe they were afraid that the horses would put them out of a job. No one knows for sure.

DOG'S BEST FRIEND

In 1801, the first fire hydrants, fed by a system of underground pipes, appeared on the streets of Philadelphia. No longer was it necessary to carry water to the scene. But the fire companies took to hiring tough guys to guard the fireplugs (hydrants) so rival units couldn't use them. These "plug-uglies" were the biggest, meanest fellows in town and didn't mind breaking a few bones to keep their rivals away. By the way, they are called fireplugs because they used to have a big wooden plug that kept the water from gushing out.

Women are firefighters, too. The first American woman firefighter on record was Molly Williams, who lived in the late 1700s. By the early 1900s there were all-woman companies like this one in Silver Spring, Maryland.

TOUGH TIMES, BIG STRIDES

In between the brawling and the bravado, some great things were happening. The 1800s brought the invention of fire bells and alarm boxes, strong rubber hoses and big steam pumpers, lightweight metal ladders…even the first chemical fire extinguishers. But every new development was greeted with scorn and took years to gain acceptance.

JUST SAY NO TO FIGHTING

In 1853, Cincinnati, Ohio, had had enough of street-fighting firefighters. They established the country's first salaried fire department. Firefighters were paid by the day, *not* by the fire, and losses to buildings and life dropped dramatically. Soon, other big cities followed suit.

IN THE SHADOW OF WAR

It took a war to bring about the next big change in the way fires were fought. When the Civil War broke out in the 1860s and so many men went off to fight, horses finally gained their place on the force. For the next 60 years, they were a valiant part of the firefighting scene. When gasoline-powered vehicles emerged at the turn of the century, there was the same resistance to change. Firefighters didn't trust them, and in truth, they were prone to breakdowns. Until the 1930s horses were *still* used to pull equipment.

Why dalmatians? Back in horse-and-buggy days, horses were always getting stolen. But if you owned a dalmatian, you had a live-in burglar alarm. These dogs love horses and protect them fiercely. When firefighters began to use horses to pull their heavy rigs, the dogs were part of the package.

Unforgettable

Fire must have been an amazing thing to early humans. It came from the sky in a hot bolt of white light that struck the trees, setting them ablaze and burning everything in its path. And yet, when it was captured it gave so much—heat on a cold day, light in the dark of night, and protection from wild animals.

But it could turn on its captors so easily.

As the centuries passed, men and women mastered fire...or thought they had. They noticed that rocks did not burn, and so they built stone fireplaces. They discovered that a spark could start a fire and so they learned to strike rocks together to create this magical force at will.

But as the great cities of the world grew, people were often reminded of just how powerful fire was. So from the time of the earliest civilizations, firefighters were around.

A.D. 64
DID ROME BURN WHILE NERO FIDDLED?

Legend has it that the mad emperor Nero played his violin while his great city burned in a fire that destroyed two-thirds of it. But at the time of the fire, the city of Rome was a mess. Nero had drawn up plans to rebuild it, with sturdier construction and plumbing. Some historians say he was merely trying to clear the way for a more modern city when the blaze got out of hand.

1666
THE GREAT FIRE OF LONDON

It started in a small house on a street called Pudding Lane where the homes were packed tightly together. When it was over five days later, 13,200 houses, 87 churches, several hospitals, libraries, and a prison had burned. Even 100,000 boats and barges along the river caught fire. More than 200,000 people were left homeless. Almost the entire city was destroyed.

1871
CHICAGO AND MRS. O'LEARY'S COW

They don't call Chicago the Windy City for nothing. Rumor has it that on the night of October 8, an unhappy cow knocked over a lantern. It had not rained in weeks and strong winds fanned the flames until 2,000 acres were on fire. Nearly 90,000 people were left homeless, and 300 people lost their lives. When it was over, 18,000 buildings—most of the city—lay in ashes.

Blazes

One of the first known brigades was in ancient Rome, started by the emperor Augustus Caesar. He ordered 600 slaves to put out any and all fires. Of course, the slaves were not thrilled with this assignment. After all, it was dangerous. After 20 years of halfhearted firefighting, the emperor created a paid force of firefighters called *Vigiles,* which means watchmen.

But huge fires still destroyed cities. These are some that became legends.

THE FIRES OF WAR

Wartime brings fire with it—fire that can destroy cities with the drop of one powerful bomb. Bombs break gas lines as well as igniting wood and paper with powerful blasts of heat. During World War II, fire was a greater danger than gunfire. London had more than 300,000 buildings burned. Dresden, Germany, was almost completely destroyed by bombs that started fires. Hiroshima and Nagasaki in Japan were all but wiped out by huge firestorms caused by atomic bombs.

During the Gulf War in the Middle East, armies set fire to huge oil refineries. It took months to get them under control.

People are far worse enemies than any wildfire.

Two World War II firefighters battle fatigue and flames.

MAN-MADE FIRES

Oil wells and drilling rigs are a firefighter's worst nightmare. In fact, there is a special breed of firefighter who specializes only in oil-rig fires. They use more than water and foam to stop a blaze. They use explosives to stop out-of-control fires. The explosions quickly consume all of the oxygen.

1906
THE SAN FRANCISCO EARTHQUAKE

Earthquakes and fire go hand in hand. And many times, the fires that start as a result of broken gas pipes and upset fireplaces cause worse damage than the movement of the earth. On April 18, as the earth trembled and split apart in northern California, fires broke out and burned wildly for two days. When it was over, 4.7 square miles of the city had burned to the ground, with 700 lives and 25,000 buildings lost.

1993
THE SOUTHERN CALIFORNIA WILDFIRES

Sometimes beautiful weather can create disasters. After weeks without rain, the city of Los Angeles found itself threatened by a fire that simply could not be stopped. More than 6,500 firefighters were called in to control it. Water from the Pacific Ocean was even hauled in by helicopter. But the fires burned for two weeks, destroyed over 1,000 homes, and caused billions of dollars in damage.

Clouds of fire like these are an almost everyday occurrence in the oil fields.

Fire has been around since before life on Earth began. It destroys whatever it touches, and yet, strangely, it also creates. The truth is, the balance of nature depends on fire. But can we find a way to control it, a way to peacefully coexist with it?

What Lies Ahead?

SMOKEY THE BEAR'S MISTAKE?

"Only YOU can prevent forest fires." That's what that famous bear with the forest ranger's hat said in posters and on TV. The U.S. Forest Service had a very strong symbol in the sweet little cub that was rescued from a bad blaze. And the message was almost right. A careless match or a poorly put out campfire is a disaster waiting to happen. But they were wrong about one thing. The forests need to burn.

Small fires have been a part of nature's plan for millions of years. *Small*—that is the important part. But for the last few years, huge wildfires, some with walls of flames hundreds of feet high, have burned millions and millions of acres. The fires have grown fiercer and more destructive each year. **FIRE ECOLOGISTS**, people who study the effect fire has on the earth, think they know the reason why.

FIRE FOOD

Wildland fires have to burn. If they don't, massive piles of dead brush and saplings (tiny trees) build up. The saplings steal food from the mature trees, and dead brush becomes a mound of kindling—the perfect fire starter for a huge blaze. In Arizona, when nature was allowed to take its course, sections of the Ponderosa pine forest used to burn every two to three years. Now some haven't burned in 20 years. Scientists have called that underbrush "a firebomb waiting to go off."

WHAT'S THE SOLUTION?

They are called **CONTROLLED BURNS**, fires that are deliberately set to imitate nature. The U.S. Forest Service is just now beginning to use controlled burns, setting small fires on windless, humid days when a blaze can be easily controlled. By the year 2015 they hope to run controlled burns on a million acres a year. And while that sounds like a lot, it's an area of only about 2,000 square miles. When you spread that over the 3.5 million square miles of the 50 states, it's a relatively small patch of land.

Where do you begin? Chemical fires can be overwhelming.

FOAM AND FIRE

As far back as the 1870s, firefighters experimented with small hand grenades made of glass. They were filled with

chemicals that would turn to a heavy vapor when they mixed with air. Those fumes were supposed to work like a blanket on the fire and smother it. They really didn't work all that well, but the idea was a good one.

Nowadays, firefighters sometimes use **FOAM** to rob a fire of its oxygen. They use it mostly for fuel and chemical fires. Oil and water don't mix. When water hits the flaming oil it spatters and erupts, spreading a fire instead of putting it out. But foam will completely blanket the flames. The only problem is, it costs a lot more than water.

In the future, chemicals may become a bigger part of the firefighting arsenal.

WHAT LIES AHEAD?

Every 52 seconds someone's home is threatened by flame. This has to change.
  Controlled burns will help to protect houses set at the edges of heavily forested areas. More powerful equipment will put out fires faster. And **FIRE ENGINEERS** will continue to come up with new ways to master fire.

SCIENCE MEETS FIRE

In today's high-tech world, one of the toughest problems facing firefighters is massive chemical fires that release deadly poisons into the air. Burning plastics are a lot harder to bring under control than wood. Scientists are researching new ways to deal with this challenge.
  Protecting firefighters from injury is another thing that engineers are working on. They are experimenting with improved turnout gear. These new coats will actually keep track of a firefighter's physical condition—monitor body temperature, pulse, even heartbeat.

When disasters such as earthquakes strike in areas with huge office buildings, the search for survivors becomes very hard. As buildings get bigger, new ways to search for survivors will have to be developed.

INTERESTED IN GETTING INVOLVED IN FIREFIGHTING?

YOU'RE CLOSER THAN YOU THINK!
When you are 12 years old, you can become a junior firefighter. The Explorer program, which is affiliated with Boy and Girl Scouts of America, works with many volunteer firefighting companies. Other community youth groups can also get involved in fire safety.

12 Things You Can Do Right Now

1. Match Madness

Don't even *think* of playing with a book of matches or a lighter that might have been left lying around. Ninety-five percent of the fires lit by kids are started with matches.

2. Outlet Overload

If you see an outlet with an "octopus" plug in it, tell your grown-ups, then yank it out. Explain that they should get a UL-approved strip outlet. And never, ever run an extension cord under a rug. The cord can fray and spark.

4. Workshop Washup

Clean up after woodworking. Sawdust and wood shavings are like delicious snacks to a hungry fire. A spark from a power saw or an electric motor can easily start a blaze.

6. Heater Horrors

A little electric or kerosene heater may seem like a harmless way to warm a room on a cold day. But these warmers can prove deadly. Keep them at least three feet from any furniture, drapes, or people. Turn them *off* before you go to sleep or leave the house. And always take extra care around them, making sure never, ever to knock them over.

3. The Careless Cook

Try to wear short sleeves when you are cooking or keep long sleeves tightly buttoned. A rolled-up sleeve could easily roll down and touch the flames.

5. Painter's Paradise

Throw out that old paint. It's gross and you're never going to use it again anyway. And it is extremely flammable. If you must save any of it, store it in airtight metal containers.

7. Detect That Smoke!

If you don't have smoke alarms in your house, nag your parents and tell them that most fatal fires occur in homes without them. There should be one outside each bedroom and at least one on each floor. If you *do* have smoke alarms, make sure you check the batteries every few months. They don't work with dead ones! CO alarms, which detect carbon monoxide in the home, are also a great idea.

8. Have a Home Fire Drill

Every school in America has fire drills. But fires are far more likely to happen in your home. Begin by getting the whole family to decide on a meeting place such as the street corner, so you will instantly be able to tell if everyone was able to get out.

9. Chimney Check

If you have a fireplace and use it often, make sure it gets cleaned by a professional *every year*. There are things happening up inside that you can't see. Soft woods (such as pine and other evergreens) leave highly flammable creosote deposits on the inside of the flue.

10. Make Your Escape

A smoke detector will let you know if there is a fire, but if you don't know what to do or where to go, you could be in big trouble. Make sure that you know of two ways to get out of each bedroom in the house. Draw an escape map of your home, and include every window and door.

11. Stay on the Lookout

Become the "fire inspector" in your house. Keep watch over your home. Remember that *you* can prevent fires from happening.

12. MAKE A FIRE KIT

Start with a **FIRE EXTINGUISHER** or two. One should be kept in the kitchen, one in the workshop or basement. Learn how to use them. There's nothing worse than trying to figure out how to use a fire extinguisher while a blaze spreads.

Next, add a few **FLASHLIGHTS**. Plug-in rechargeable ones are a good idea. With them you don't have to worry about batteries running low.

Include your **ESCAPE MAPS** and go over them every six months with everyone in the family. Knowing how to get out in a hurry is important.

SAFETY LADDERS are a must if you live in a multilevel home. They hook onto the window-sills and let you get out through a window if the doorways are blocked. Practice using them. They take some getting used to.

If You'd Like to Learn More

MAGAZINES AND BOOKS

The following magazines are written for firefighters and chiefs, but they are packed with wonderful photos and stories that all can enjoy. Write directly to them to get subscription information, or check your public library.

FIRE CHIEF MAGAZINE
Hallmark Data Systems
6201 Westhoward
Niles, IL 60714
(847) 647-1200

FIRE ENGINEERING
P.O. Box 1289
Tulsa, OK 74101
(918) 835-3161

FIREHOUSE
82 Firehouse Lane
Box 52824
Boulder, Colorado 80322

The following books are also highly recommended:

THE GREAT FIRE
by Jim Murphy
Scholastic, 1995

For older readers:
RESCUERS IN ACTION
by Barry Smith
Moseby Lifeline, 1996

YOUNG MEN AND FIRE
by Norman Maclean
The University of Chicago Press, 1992

WHERE TO WRITE

These organizations deal with different aspects of firefighting. Write directly to them to get more information.

INTERNATIONAL ASSOCIATION OF FIRE CHIEFS
Where fire chiefs go when they need answers.
4025 Fair Ridge Drive
Fairfax, VA 22033

THE NATIONAL FIRE PROTECTION AGENCY
A good source for home fire safety information.
NFPA Public Affairs Office
Dept. FH
Battery March Park
Quincy, MA 02269

WOMEN IN THE FIRE SERVICE
Deals specifically with women firefighters.
P.O. Box 5446
Madison, WI 53705

PLACES TO VISIT

Many states have fire museums that are open to the public. With antique trucks and gear, they are wonderful places to spend some time. There are more than 150 in the U.S., located in over 40 states. For more information, check out:

DISCOVERING AMERICA'S FIRE MUSEUMS
Compiled and edited by W. Fred Conway
FBH Publishers

FILMS ABOUT FIRE

The following films offer a Hollywood view of firefighting—not always accurate but always interesting.

ALWAYS (1989)
Rated PG. A high-flying firefighter returns from the dead to teach a rookie pilot. A remake of a classic film called *A Guy Named Joe.*

BACKDRAFT (1991)
Rated R. Two brothers from a family of firefighters match wits with an arsonist. Three Academy Award nominations.

HELLFIGHTERS (1968)
Rated G. John Wayne stars as the head of a team of crack oil-well firefighters.

THE TOWERING INFERNO (1974)
Rated PG. Fire breaks out at the top of a San Francisco skyscraper. Acadamy Award winner for Best Cinematography, among others.

ONLINE RESOURCES

There are excellent web sites about fire, many maintained by fire departments around the country. This address will take you to most of them:

http://www.excaliber.com/fire/firelin1.htm links you to departments in almost every state. The Los Angeles Fire Department site is especially good.

PHOTO CREDITS

Page 1: Securitex/ImageAde.

Pages 2–3: Gene Levins.

Pages 4–5: left, Scott Aviation; top right, Rick Sheyvada; middle right, Bettmann Archive; bottom center, Jack Reznicki; bottom right, Photodisc.

Pages 6–7: left, MSA; center, Corel; badge, Blackington; gloves, Jack Reznicki; far right, Corel.

Pages 8–9: background, matches, candle, Photodisc; top right, Liaison; center bottom, Jack Reznicki.

Pages 10–11: helmet, Cairns and Bros; SCBA, Scott Aviation; searchlight, Streamlight Flashlights; boots, walkie-talkies, rope, firefighter, Jack Reznicki; fire tool, T-N-T Firetools; alarm, MSA; protective clothing, Securitex/ImageAde.

Pages 12–13: left, MSA; center, Securitex/ImageAde; top right, Photodisc; bottom right, Corbis; middle right, MSA.

Pages 14–15: pumper, rescue truck, purple truck, KME Trucks; snorkel, TC; haz-mat, Central States Fire Apparatus/Ovendon Wheeler; aerial, Check Six.

Pages 16–17: left, Akron Brass; center and bottom right, Jack Reznicki; right, Barry Smith.

Pages 18–19: all pictures, Barry Smith except: fire boat and airplane, Liaison.

Pages 20–21: top left, top far right, Hurst; bottom left, Barry Smith; center right, Manfred Vetter; bottom right, MSA; center left, Paratech.

Pages 22–23: top left, top right, Photodisc; center left, Corbis; center right, Jack Reznicki; bottom center, Corel.

Pages 24–25: all pictures, Jack Reznicki except: apparatus, Corel; food, Photodisc

Pages 26–27: all pictures, Barry Smith except: swift-water rescue (far left), Rick Sheyveda.

Pages 28–29: top left, bottom left, center right, far right center, Liaison; bottom right, Richard Mangen; all others, Photodisc.

Pages 30–31: bottom left, The Stock Market; far right center, Jack Reznicki; ambulance, Corel; all others, Photodisc.

Pages 32–33: bottom left, Jack Reznicki; far and bottom right, Bureau of Alcohol, Tobacco and Firearms; all others, Photodisc.

Page 34: far left, Corel; center left, MSA.

Page 35: all, Jack Reznicki.

Pages 36–37: center, Williamsburg, VA; all others, collection of Henry Bergson.

Pages 38–39: center, Bettmann Archive; women firefighters, Corbis; dog, TC; antique extinguisher, Photodisc; hydrant, Brian Michaud.

Pages 40–41: Nero, San Francisco, Bettmann Archive; London, Henry Bergson; cow, Photodisc; wildfire fighter, Barry Smith; WWII firefighters, Corbis; refinery fire, Photodisc.

Pages 42–43: left top, Corbis; forest fire, industrial fire, Liaison; far top, middle right, Henry Bergson; bottom center, Corel.

Pages 44–45: all pictures, Photodisc except: bottom left, Jack Reznicki.

THE AUTHOR WISHES TO THANK:
Steve Grasha at MSA,
manufacturers of air cylinders and breathing apparatus;
Jess Finefrock at AKRON BRASS,
makers of nozzles;
Phil Gerace at KME FIRE APPARATUS,
manufacturers of fire trucks;
Gregory Fitts at SAULSBURY FIRE AND RESCUE,
manufacturers of fire trucks;
Ross Cochren at SECURITEX,
makers of protective clothing;
Michael Lo Carlo at CAIRNS & BROTHERS,
makers of protective clothing and fire suppression equipment;
Harold Boer at CENTRAL STATES FIRE APPARATUS,
makers of trucks;
Mark Trujillo at TNT FIRE TOOLS,
makers of forced entry equipment;
MANFRED VETTER GMBH,
makers of inflatables;
Rita Byron at HALE PRODUCTS/HURST RESCUE TOOLS, *makers of rescue equipment;*
STREAMLIGHT-FLASHLIGHTS,
manufacturers of searchlights;
CMC RESCUE EQUIPMENT;
Jeff Berend at RESCUE MAGAZINE;
Richard J. Mangan and Wayne Williams at Northern Region Regional Office
USDA FOREST SERVICE MTDC.

A NOTE FROM THE AUTHOR

Several years ago, I was drafted into service as a Cub Scout den leader. Within a year I had inherited the cochairmanship of a 60-boy pack along with my 14-boy den. It was during this time that I fell in with the firefighters of the Golden's Bridge Fire Department, our sponsor group. What great people they are!

Inspired by their selfless dedication to our community and also inspired by the freshness and curiosity of all those young Scouts, I set out to capture as much of the excitement of firefighting as I could.

As I researched the profession and suited up with a fire department, my excitement grew.

I have been in the business of communicating for almost 20 years as an art director and writer. But this has been the most thrilling assignment of my entire career.

If just a few young people, inspired by the tales told in this book, choose to become firefighters—either volunteer or paid—it will prove to be one of the sweetest accomplishments of my life.

A SPECIAL WORD OF THANKS

This book could not have been written without the help of the following people. Thanks for sharing your thrilling stories.

Patrick O'Conner and the Golden's Bridge (NY) Fire Department

Bart McCleary, Kevin Plank, Tom McNulty, and the firefighters of the Danbury (CT) Fire Department

Jeff Giordano of the New York City (NY) Fire Department

Barry D. Smith of the Santa Clara (CA) Fire Department

Dan Taylor and Jake Gershen of the South Salem (NY) Fire Department

Karen Barber of the Lewisboro (NY) Ambulance Corps

Hank Bergson of Fire Antiquities in Katonah, New York

Thanks also to our expert readers: Michael Forgy, Project Coordinator, IEMS Program at the International Association of Fire Chiefs, and Steve Carter of the Maryland Fire and Rescue Institute.

And last but not least, with love and gratitude to Lou, Alex, and Tish Scolnik for believing in me and to the boys and girls of Cub Scout Pack 154 and Brownie Troop 2340 for inspiring me.

A

accelerants (fire intensifiers), 32
aerial trucks, 15
air guns (rescue tools), 20
airboats, 19
airplanes, 19, 28, 29
ambulances, 15, 31
apparatus; *see* fire trucks; rescue trucks
arson
    defined, 32
    six types of, 33
arson investigators, 32–33
ATF (Arson Task Force), 33
ATF (Bureau of Alcohol, Tobacco and Firearms), 33
attack lines (hoses), 16, 17, 25

B

backdraft, 9
boats, 18–19, 27
boots, 11, 12, 34, 35
Boy and Girl Scouts of America, 43
bucket brigades, 36–37, 41
bunker pants, 11, 12–13

C

campfires, as fire hazards, 42
cave rescues, 27
CFIs (Certified Fire Investigators), 33
chains (fireline sections), 29
chemical fires, 43
chemical spills, 6, 13, 14
chemicals, for use in firefighting, 29, 39, 41, 43
Chicago fire, 40
chief's car, 15
chimneys, as fire hazards, 45
cleanup kits, 13
CO (carbon monoxide) alarms, 45
collapse rescues, 27
confined-space rescues, 27
controlled burns, 42
cooking, as fire hazard, 44
CPR (cardiopulmonary resuscitation), 31
cutters (rescue tools), 20

D

dalmatians, 39
delay devices (fire inhibitors), 32
discharge lines (hoses), 16, 25
dispatch (radio), 25
dogs
    as arson investigators, 33
    as firehouse pets, 39

E

earthquakes, and fire, 41
emergency procedures, 30–31
EMS (Emergency Medical Service), 30–31
EMTs (Emergency Medical Technicians), 30–31
escape procedures, 9, 45
explosives, for use in firefighting, 41

F

fear; *see* firefighters, feelings of
fire
    four parts of, 9,
    three ingredients of, 8, 9, 29
fire boats, 18
fire drills, 45
fire ecologists, 42
fire engineers, 43
fire engines; *see* fire trucks
fire extinguishers, 39, 45

fire gases, 9
fire hazards, at home, 44–45
fire hydrants, 38
fire marshal, 32
fire prevention, at home, 44–45
fire tools; 11, 12–13, 32; *see also* firefighting gear
fire trucks, 14–15, 16–17, 24–25, 37, 39
Firefighter McNulty's Four-Alarm Chicken (recipe), 25
firefighters
    feelings of, 6–7, 17, 21, 24–25, 34–35
    junior, 43
    as professionals, 23, 39
    school for, 29
    and teamwork, 11, 26, 27, 29, 34
    test to become, 35
    as volunteers, 22, 36, 37
    women as, 38
    see also EMTs; hotshots; smoke jumpers
firefighting, history of, 36–41, 43
firefighting gear, 10–13, 28–29, 34; *see also* haz-mat gear; rescue gear; turnout gear
firehouses; *see* station houses
firelines, 29
fireplaces; *see* chimneys, as fire hazards
fireplugs; *see* fire hydrants
first-aid training, 30
flame, as part of fire, 9
flash point, 8, 9
flashlights, 10, 45
flashover, 9, 34
foam; *see* chemicals, for use in firefighting
forest fires, 28–29, 42
Franklin, Benjamin, 37, 38
friction, and fire, 8
fuel, as fire ingredient, 8, 9, 29

H

Hand-in-Hand (insurance) Company, 37, 38
haz-mat (hazardous-materials) gear, 13
haz-mat (hazardous-materials) truck, 14
heat
    as fire ingredient, 8, 9, 29
    as part of fire, 9, 34
heaters, as fire hazards, 44
heat-seeking cameras; *see* TICs
helicopters, 19, 29, 41
helmets, 10, 12–13, 31, 34
hook-and-ladder trucks; *see* aerial trucks
horses, used in firefighting, 38, 39
hoses, 16–17, 25, 32, 35, 39
hotshots, 28–29
hovercrafts, 18

I

inflatables (rescue tools), 21
intake lines (hoses), 16

J

Jaws of life, 20–21
Jefferson, Thomas, 37
jet ski; *see* PWC

L

lightning, and fire, 28
London, Great Fire of, 40

M

matches, as fire hazards, 8, 32, 42, 44
mine rescues, 27
monitors (for hoses), 17

N

911 (emergency telephone number), 25, 30

O

oil-well fires, 41
O'Leary's, Mrs., cow, 40
outlets, as fire hazards, 44
oxygen, as fire ingredient, 8, 9, 29, 43

P

paint, as fire hazard, 44
paramedic, 30
PASS (Personal Alert Safety System), 11
point of origin, of fire, 33
portable water tank, 16
professional firefighters, 23, 39
Pulaskis (fire tools), 29
pumper trucks, 14, 16–17
PWC (Personal Water Craft), 18

R

rams (rescue tools), 20
rescue gear, 20–21, 31; *see also* turnout gear
rescue trucks, 14–15, 31; *see also* fire trucks
rescue workers; *see* EMTs; firefighters
Revere, Paul, 37
Rome, burning of, 40
rope rescues, 26
ropes, 10, 26, 27, 31, 36

S

safety ladders, 45
San Francisco earthquake and fire, 41
sawdust, as fire hazard, 44
SCBA (Self-Contained Breathing Apparatus), 10, 12–13
search-and-rescue teams, 25; *see also* USAR teams
shake 'n' bakes (fireproof tents), 29
silvers (airport firefighting gear), 13
skeds (stretchers), 27
sky Jell-O; *see* chemicals, for use in firefighting
smoke
    as firefighting hazard, 9, 21, 25, 35
    as part of fire, 9
smoke alarms, 45
smoke-jumper school, 29
smoke jumpers, 28–29
Smokey the Bear, 42
snorkel trucks, 15
southern California wildfires, 41
station houses, 24
swift-water rescues, 26

T

tenders (inflatable boats), 27
TICs (Thermal-Imaging Cameras), 21
trucks; *see* fire trucks; rescue trucks
turnout gear, 11, 12–13, 28, 34, 43

U

Union Fire Company (Philadelphia), 37
U.S. Forest Service, 28, 29, 42
USAR (Urban Search and Rescue) teams, 27

V

volunteer firefighters, 22, 36, 37

W

walkie-talkies, 11, 12–13, 31
war, and fire, 39, 41
Washington, George, 37
water rescues, 18–19, 27; *see also* swift-water rescues
wetbikes; *see* PWC
wildfires, 41; *see also* forest fires
women, as firefighters, 38
wood shavings, as fire hazard, 44

Deleted From
Peterson Library

WHEATLAND scanning Library
1850 W. 103RD ST.
NAPERVILLE, IL 60564